Hudson Music®
presents

DRUM LESSON PLANNER

Developed by Hudson Music's Teacher Integration Program (TIP)™

This book belongs to: _____

Dates of lessons from_____to_____

Catalog HDBK21/HL006620136
ISBN: 1423471342

HUDSON MUSIC®

To view downloadable clips and more educational information, vist:
www.hudsonmusic.com

ELEMENTS OF MUSIC

Here is a review of basic music notation for you and your teacher to use for reference.

The Staff

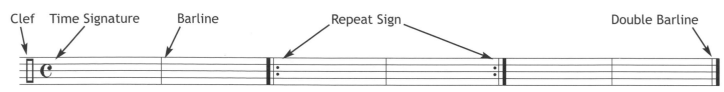

Music is notated on a staff of five lines, which is divided into sections called **measures**. The measures are separated by **barlines**. A **repeat sign** means to repeat the measures between the signs. A **double barline** indicates the end of a piece. The **clef** indicates how the music should be read. Percussion usually uses a neutral clef (shown). The **time signature** explains how to count the music (see below).

Note and Rest Values

The duration of musical sounds is indicated by **notes** and **rests**. Notes represent sounds of a specific length, and rests represent silence of a specific length. This is what the notes and rests look like:

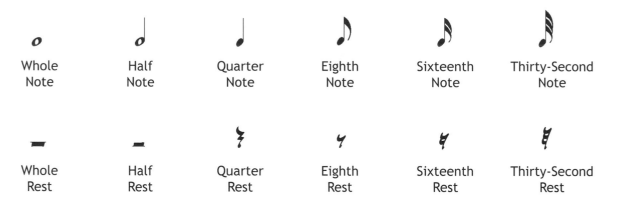

| Whole Note | Half Note | Quarter Note | Eighth Note | Sixteenth Note | Thirty-Second Note |

| Whole Rest | Half Rest | Quarter Rest | Eighth Rest | Sixteenth Rest | Thirty-Second Rest |

The following charts show the relative value of the notes and rests:

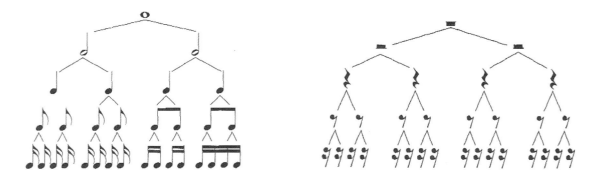

Time Signature

The time signature explains how to count the music. The top number tells you the number of beats in the measure, and the bottom number tells you the type of note that gets one beat. In this case, there are four beats in the measure, and the quarter note gets one beat. A convenient way to memorize this is to remember that there are four quarter notes in a measure of 4/4. If, for example, we change the time signature to 5/8, then there would be five eighth notes in the measure.

DRUM NOTATION

Here is a key you can use for reference when writing out your own drum patterns. This key shows most of the instruments that you would need to notate on the drumset. It conforms to the Percussive Arts Society standard for drumset notation and is used in many Hudson Music books, as well as *Modern Drummer* magazine.

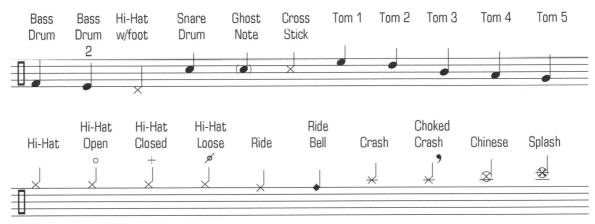

CHART READING

Here are some of the most common musical notation elements you will encounter on drum charts:

Slash Notation

Tells you to play any groove that fits the style/song.

Ensemble Figures

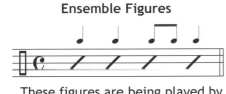

These figures are being played by another instrument in the band and are optional.

Two-bar Repeat

Repeat the previous two measures.

Rhythmic Notation

Figures written this way are meant to be played by the entire band.

One-Bar Repeat

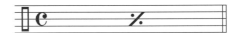

Repeat the previous measure.

First and Second Endings

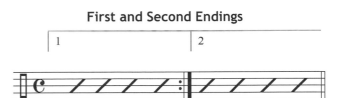

First play the first ending and go back to the last repeat sign. On the second time through, skip the first ending and play the second.

D.C. (Da Capo): go back to the beginning of the chart.

D.S. (Dal Segno): go back to the sign 𝄋.

To Coda: go to the coda (a separate ending at the bottom of the chart), represented by ⊕.

Al Fine: Play to the end (fine).

Letters (A, B, C, etc.) identify various sections of the song.

For more information about the Percussive Arts Society, please visit www.pas.org. Reprinted by permission of PAS.

PERCUSSIVE ARTS SOCIETY INTERNATIONAL DRUM RUDIMENTS

ALL RUDIMENTS SHOULD BE PRACTICED: OPEN (SLOW) TO CLOSE (FAST) TO OPEN (SLOW) AND/OR AT AN EVEN MODERATE MARCH TEMPO.

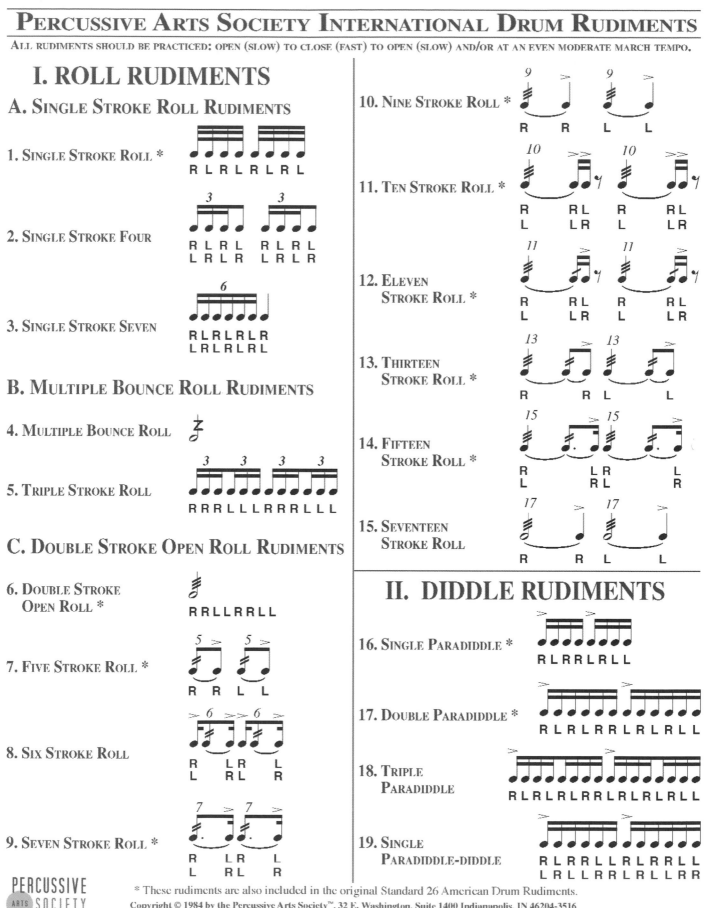

I. ROLL RUDIMENTS

A. SINGLE STROKE ROLL RUDIMENTS

1. SINGLE STROKE ROLL *
R L R L R L R L

2. SINGLE STROKE FOUR
R L R L   R L R L
L R L R   L R L R

3. SINGLE STROKE SEVEN
R L R L R L R
L R L R L R L

B. MULTIPLE BOUNCE ROLL RUDIMENTS

4. MULTIPLE BOUNCE ROLL

5. TRIPLE STROKE ROLL
R R R L L L R R R L L L

C. DOUBLE STROKE OPEN ROLL RUDIMENTS

6. DOUBLE STROKE OPEN ROLL *
R R L L R R L L

7. FIVE STROKE ROLL *
R R L L

8. SIX STROKE ROLL
R   L R   L
L   R L   R

9. SEVEN STROKE ROLL *
R   L R   L
L   R L   R

10. NINE STROKE ROLL *
R   R L   L

11. TEN STROKE ROLL *
R   R L   R   R L
L   L R   L   L R

12. ELEVEN STROKE ROLL *
R   R L   R   R L
L   L R   L   L R

13. THIRTEEN STROKE ROLL *
R   R L   L

14. FIFTEEN STROKE ROLL *
R   L R   L
L   R L   R

15. SEVENTEEN STROKE ROLL
R   R L   L

II. DIDDLE RUDIMENTS

16. SINGLE PARADIDDLE *
R L R R L R L L

17. DOUBLE PARADIDDLE *
R L R L R R L R L R L L

18. TRIPLE PARADIDDLE
R L R L R L R R L R L R L R L L

19. SINGLE PARADIDDLE-DIDDLE
R L R R L L R L R R L L
L R L L R R L R L L R R

PERCUSSIVE ARTS SOCIETY

Copyright © 1984 by the Percussive Arts Society™, 32 E. Washington, Suite 1400 Indianapolis, IN 46204-3516
International Copyright Secured   All Rights Reserved

PAS INTERNATIONAL DRUM RUDIMENTS page 2

III. FLAM RUDIMENTS

20. FLAM *

21. FLAM ACCENT *

22. FLAM TAP *

23. FLAMACUE *

24. FLAM PARADIDDLE *

25. SINGLE FLAMMED MILL

26. FLAM PARADIDDLE-DIDDLE *

27. PATAFLAFLA

28. SWISS ARMY TRIPLET

29. INVERTED FLAM TAP

30. FLAM DRAG

IV. DRAG RUDIMENTS

31. DRAG *

32. SINGLE DRAG TAP *

33. DOUBLE DRAG TAP *

34. LESSON 25 *

35. SINGLE DRAGDIDDLE

36. DRAG PARADIDDLE #1 *

37. DRAG PARADIDDLE #2 *

38. SINGLE RATAMACUE *

39. DOUBLE RATAMACUE *

40. TRIPLE RATAMACUE *

LONG-TERM PLANS & GOALS

LONG-TERM PLANS & GOALS

LONG-TERM PLANS & GOALS

_____

_____

_____

_____

_____

_____

_____

_____

_____

_____

_____

_____

_____

_____

_____

_____

_____

_____

_____

_____

DATE: _____

ASSIGNMENTS:

BOOK   PAGE(S)   SPECIAL INSTRUCTIONS

_____   _____   _____

_____   _____   _____

_____   _____   _____

_____   _____   _____

_____   _____   _____

_____   _____   _____

DVD   CHAP(S)   SPECIAL INSTRUCTIONS

_____   _____   _____

_____   _____   _____

_____   _____   _____

WEBSITES/OTHER:_____

_____

RECOMMENDED
LISTENING:_____

_____

DATE: _____

ASSIGNMENTS:

BOOK   PAGE(S)   SPECIAL INSTRUCTIONS

_____   _____   _____

_____   _____   _____

_____   _____   _____

_____   _____   _____

_____   _____   _____

_____   _____   _____

DVD   CHAP(S)   SPECIAL INSTRUCTIONS

_____   _____   _____

_____   _____   _____

_____   _____   _____

WEBSITES/OTHER:_____

_____

RECOMMENDED
LISTENING:_____

_____

DATE: _____

ASSIGNMENTS:

BOOK	PAGE(S)	SPECIAL INSTRUCTIONS
_____	_____	_____
_____	_____	_____
_____	_____	_____
_____	_____	_____
_____	_____	_____
_____	_____	_____

DVD	CHAP(S)	SPECIAL INSTRUCTIONS
_____	_____	_____
_____	_____	_____
_____	_____	_____

WEBSITES/OTHER:_____

_____

RECOMMENDED
LISTENING:_____

_____

DATE: _____

ASSIGNMENTS:

BOOK   PAGE(S)   SPECIAL INSTRUCTIONS

_____   _____   _____

_____   _____   _____

_____   _____   _____

_____   _____   _____

_____   _____   _____

DVD   CHAP(S)   SPECIAL INSTRUCTIONS

_____   _____   _____

_____   _____   _____

_____   _____   _____

WEBSITES/OTHER:_____

_____

RECOMMENDED
LISTENING:_____

_____

DATE: _____

ASSIGNMENTS:

BOOK   PAGE(S)   SPECIAL INSTRUCTIONS

_____   _____   _____

_____   _____   _____

_____   _____   _____

_____   _____   _____

_____   _____   _____

DVD   CHAP(S)   SPECIAL INSTRUCTIONS

_____   _____   _____

_____   _____   _____

_____   _____   _____

WEBSITES/OTHER:_____

_____

RECOMMENDED
LISTENING:_____

_____

DATE: _____

ASSIGNMENTS:

BOOK   PAGE(S)   SPECIAL INSTRUCTIONS

_____   _____   _____

_____   _____   _____

_____   _____   _____

_____   _____   _____

_____   _____   _____

DVD   CHAP(S)   SPECIAL INSTRUCTIONS

_____   _____   _____

_____   _____   _____

_____   _____   _____

WEBSITES/OTHER:_____

_____

RECOMMENDED
LISTENING:_____

_____

DATE: _____

ASSIGNMENTS:

BOOK   PAGE(S) SPECIAL INSTRUCTIONS

_____ _____ _____

_____ _____ _____

_____ _____ _____

_____ _____ _____

_____ _____ _____

DVD   CHAP(S) SPECIAL INSTRUCTIONS

_____ _____ _____

_____ _____ _____

_____ _____ _____

WEBSITES/OTHER:_____

_____

RECOMMENDED
LISTENING:_____

_____

DATE: _____

ASSIGNMENTS:

BOOK   PAGE(S)   SPECIAL INSTRUCTIONS

_____   _____   _____

_____   _____   _____

_____   _____   _____

_____   _____   _____

_____   _____   _____

DVD   CHAP(S)   SPECIAL INSTRUCTIONS

_____   _____   _____

_____   _____   _____

_____   _____   _____

WEBSITES/OTHER:_____

_____

RECOMMENDED
LISTENING:_____

_____

DATE: _____

ASSIGNMENTS:

BOOK   PAGE(S)   SPECIAL INSTRUCTIONS

_____   _____   _____

_____   _____   _____

_____   _____   _____

_____   _____   _____

_____   _____   _____

DVD   CHAP(S)   SPECIAL INSTRUCTIONS

_____   _____   _____

_____   _____   _____

_____   _____   _____

WEBSITES/OTHER:_____

_____

RECOMMENDED
LISTENING:_____

_____

DATE: _____

ASSIGNMENTS:

BOOK   PAGE(S)   SPECIAL INSTRUCTIONS

_____   _____   _____

_____   _____   _____

_____   _____   _____

_____   _____   _____

_____   _____   _____

DVD   CHAP(S)   SPECIAL INSTRUCTIONS

_____   _____   _____

_____   _____   _____

_____   _____   _____

WEBSITES/OTHER:_____

_____

RECOMMENDED
LISTENING:_____

_____

DATE: _____

ASSIGNMENTS:

BOOK	PAGE(S)	SPECIAL INSTRUCTIONS
_____	_____	_____
_____	_____	_____
_____	_____	_____
_____	_____	_____
_____	_____	_____
_____	_____	_____

DVD	CHAP(S)	SPECIAL INSTRUCTIONS
_____	_____	_____
_____	_____	_____
_____	_____	_____

WEBSITES/OTHER:_____

_____

RECOMMENDED
LISTENING:_____

_____

DATE: _____

ASSIGNMENTS:

BOOK   PAGE(S)   SPECIAL INSTRUCTIONS

_____ _____ _____

_____ _____ _____

_____ _____ _____

_____ _____ _____

_____ _____ _____

_____ _____ _____

DVD   CHAP(S)   SPECIAL INSTRUCTIONS

_____ _____ _____

_____ _____ _____

_____ _____ _____

WEBSITES/OTHER:_____

_____

RECOMMENDED
LISTENING:_____

_____

DATE: _____

ASSIGNMENTS:

BOOK   PAGE(S)   SPECIAL INSTRUCTIONS

_____

_____

_____

_____

_____

DVD   CHAP(S)   SPECIAL INSTRUCTIONS

_____

_____

_____

WEBSITES/OTHER:_____

_____

RECOMMENDED
LISTENING:_____

_____

DATE: _____

ASSIGNMENTS:

BOOK   PAGE(S)   SPECIAL INSTRUCTIONS

_____   _____   _____

_____   _____   _____

_____   _____   _____

_____   _____   _____

_____   _____   _____

DVD   CHAP(S)   SPECIAL INSTRUCTIONS

_____   _____   _____

_____   _____   _____

_____   _____   _____

WEBSITES/OTHER:_____

_____

RECOMMENDED
LISTENING:_____

_____

DATE: _____

ASSIGNMENTS:

BOOK   PAGE(S)   SPECIAL INSTRUCTIONS

_____   _____   _____

_____   _____   _____

_____   _____   _____

_____   _____   _____

_____   _____   _____

DVD   CHAP(S)   SPECIAL INSTRUCTIONS

_____   _____   _____

_____   _____   _____

_____   _____   _____

WEBSITES/OTHER:_____

_____

RECOMMENDED
LISTENING:_____

_____

DATE: _____

ASSIGNMENTS:

BOOK   PAGE(S)   SPECIAL INSTRUCTIONS

_____   _____   _____

_____   _____   _____

_____   _____   _____

_____   _____   _____

_____   _____   _____

_____   _____   _____

DVD   CHAP(S)   SPECIAL INSTRUCTIONS

_____   _____   _____

_____   _____   _____

_____   _____   _____

WEBSITES/OTHER:_____

_____

RECOMMENDED
LISTENING:_____

_____

DATE: _____

ASSIGNMENTS:

BOOK	PAGE(S)	SPECIAL INSTRUCTIONS
_____	_____	_____
_____	_____	_____
_____	_____	_____
_____	_____	_____
_____	_____	_____

DVD	CHAP(S)	SPECIAL INSTRUCTIONS
_____	_____	_____
_____	_____	_____
_____	_____	_____

WEBSITES/OTHER:_____

_____

RECOMMENDED
LISTENING:_____

_____

DATE: _____

ASSIGNMENTS:

BOOK   PAGE(S)   SPECIAL INSTRUCTIONS

_____   _____   _____

_____   _____   _____

_____   _____   _____

_____   _____   _____

_____   _____   _____

DVD   CHAP(S)   SPECIAL INSTRUCTIONS

_____   _____   _____

_____   _____   _____

_____   _____   _____

WEBSITES/OTHER:_____

_____

RECOMMENDED
LISTENING:_____

_____

DATE: _____

ASSIGNMENTS:

BOOK   PAGE(S)   SPECIAL INSTRUCTIONS

_____   _____   _____

_____   _____   _____

_____   _____   _____

_____   _____   _____

_____   _____   _____

_____   _____   _____

DVD   CHAP(S)   SPECIAL INSTRUCTIONS

_____   _____   _____

_____   _____   _____

_____   _____   _____

WEBSITES/OTHER:_____

_____

RECOMMENDED
LISTENING:_____

_____

DATE: _____

ASSIGNMENTS:

BOOK   PAGE(S)   SPECIAL INSTRUCTIONS

_____   _____   _____

_____   _____   _____

_____   _____   _____

_____   _____   _____

_____   _____   _____

DVD   CHAP(S)   SPECIAL INSTRUCTIONS

_____   _____   _____

_____   _____   _____

_____   _____   _____

WEBSITES/OTHER:_____

_____

RECOMMENDED
LISTENING:_____

_____

DATE: _____

ASSIGNMENTS:

BOOK   PAGE(S)   SPECIAL INSTRUCTIONS

_____   _____   _____

_____   _____   _____

_____   _____   _____

_____   _____   _____

_____   _____   _____

DVD   CHAP(S)   SPECIAL INSTRUCTIONS

_____   _____   _____

_____   _____   _____

_____   _____   _____

WEBSITES/OTHER:_____

_____

RECOMMENDED
LISTENING:_____

_____

DATE: _____

ASSIGNMENTS:

BOOK   PAGE(S)   SPECIAL INSTRUCTIONS

_____   _____   _____

_____   _____   _____

_____   _____   _____

_____   _____   _____

_____   _____   _____

_____   _____   _____

DVD   CHAP(S)   SPECIAL INSTRUCTIONS

_____   _____   _____

_____   _____   _____

_____   _____   _____

WEBSITES/OTHER:_____

_____

RECOMMENDED
LISTENING:_____

_____

_____ has successfully
completed the lessons in this planner.

_____
Teacher

_____
Parent

TEACHER INTEGRATION PROGRAM

The mission of the Hudson Music Teacher Integration Program, or TIP, is to further and enhance drum education by encouraging the use of New Media by drum educators (in both private and public settings) and by offering suggestions and methods for incorporating these tools into their teaching practices. This will be done through the development of Teacher's Guides for new media, as well as print and electronic distribution of TIP support materials, and interactive online participation from TIP members and the drumming community at large. An important component will be the formation of and input from a TIP Advisory Board, whose members will be chosen from a wide variety of musical styles, geographic locations, and teaching practices.

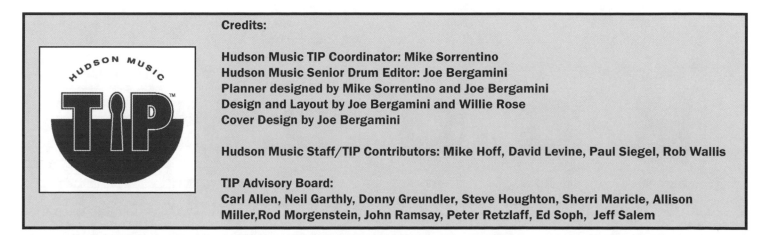

Credits:

Hudson Music TIP Coordinator: Mike Sorrentino
Hudson Music Senior Drum Editor: Joe Bergamini
Planner designed by Mike Sorrentino and Joe Bergamini
Design and Layout by Joe Bergamini and Willie Rose
Cover Design by Joe Bergamini

Hudson Music Staff/TIP Contributors: Mike Hoff, David Levine, Paul Siegel, Rob Wallis

TIP Advisory Board:
Carl Allen, Neil Garthly, Donny Greundler, Steve Houghton, Sherri Maricle, Allison Miller,Rod Morgenstein, John Ramsay, Peter Retzlaff, Ed Soph, Jeff Salem